Longman Str
Stage 6

Modern

Edited by G. C. Thornley

Illustrated by V. J. Bertoglio

Longman

Longman Group UK Limited,
Longman House, Burnt Mill, Harlow,
Essex CM20 2JE, England
and Associated Companies throughout the world.

This edition © Longman Group Limited 1967

All rights reserved; no part of this publication
may be reproduced, stored in a retrieval system
or transmitted in any form or by any means, electronic,
mechanical, photocopying, recording, or otherwise,
without the prior written permission of the Publishers.

First published 1967
This impression 1989

Acknowledgement
Cover photograph by Philip Hale

Produced by Longman Group (FE) Ltd
Printed in Hong Kong

ISBN 0-582-53777-0

Longman Structural Readers

It is today widely held that it is the structure of a language, rather than the vocabulary, which causes the greatest difficulty to the foreign learner. The supplementary readers in this series are therefore based on the principles of structure control.

Up-to-date English courses have, at each stage, a certain common content of sentence-patterns. This common content, which will be familiar to the learner at the end of each stage, is represented in the structure tables developed to govern the preparation of the series (see *A Handbook to Longman Structural Readers* for the structure tables and basic vocabulary).

Control of vocabulary is also maintained (as in many existing series of supplementary readers) and one new principle has been introduced. Content words outside the given basic vocabulary but of value in the story are introduced freely within the structural limits by a prescribed process of repetition.

The learner's pleasure in reading is thus increased, and with the strict control of useful structures, the development of a sense of achievement will be aided and the maximum value derived from the practice of supplementary reading.

Other titles at Stage 6 of Longman Structural Readers

Key to figures
1 Recommended for use with children (aged 8-12)
2 Recommended for use with young people (aged 12-15)
3 Recommended for use with older people (aged 16 plus)
 No figure: Recommended for use with all ages

General Fiction
Brave New World
 Aldous Huxley (3)
Cider with Rosie *(Overseas only)*
 Laurie Lee
The Go-Between
 L P Hartley
The L-Shaped Room
 Lynne Reid Banks
Strike the Father Dead
 John Wain

Short Stories
For Your Eyes Only
 Ian Fleming (2.3)
Modern Short Stories
 Ed G C Thornley

Non Fiction
The Kon-Tiki Expedition
 Thor Heyrdahl (2.3)

Contents

		Page
1	The Dream *Frank Tilsley*	1
2	Dark they were with Golden Eyes *Ray Bradbury*	8
3	It happened near a Lake *John Collier*	25
4	The Ugly American and the Ugly Sarkhanese *W. J. Lederer and E. Burdick*	34
5	Hilary's Aunt *Cyril Hare*	48
6	Two Weeks beyond Shoreditch *Robert Rubens*	54

Acknowledgments

We are grateful to the following for permission to include abridged and simplified versions of their copyright material:

Mrs. A. A. Gordon Clark for 'The Euthanasia of Hilary's Aunt' by Cyril Hare from *Some Like Them Dead* edited by Roy Vickers; Victor Gollancz Ltd and W. W. Norton & Co. Inc. for 'The Ugly American and the Ugly Sarkhanese' from *The Ugly American* by William J. Lederer and Eugene Burdick, Copyright © 1958 by William J. Lederer and Eugene Burdick; A. D. Peters & Co. for 'Dark They Were and Golden Eyed' by Ray Bradbury, and 'It Happened Near a Lake' by John Collier; the author's agents for 'Two Weeks Beyond Shoreditch' by Robert Rubens, Copyright © 1963 by Macmillan & Co. Ltd, and Mrs. F. Tilsley for 'The Dream' by Frank Tilsley, from *Did It Happen?* published by Oldbourne Press Ltd.

THE DREAM
Frank Tilsley

Frank Tilsley (born 1904) has done many different kinds of work during his life. He served in the Royal Air Force during the 1939 war. He was born in the north of England, but prefers now to live in the south. He has spoken on the radio on a variety of subjects. He likes gardening, walking and reading history.

His first book appeared in 1933, and since then he has written numbers of others. Among them we may mention *I'd Hate to be Dead* (1938), *Love Story of Gilbert Bright* (1940), *The Lady in the Fur Coat* (1941), and *Thicker than Water* (1955). *Boys of Coastal* (short stories) appeared in 1944.

This short story is about driving a car across Europe, and about one of the dangers that may arise on such a journey. In England, all cars keep to the left of the road, but in Europe and America they keep to the right-hand side. In Europe and America, therefore, cars have the driving wheel on the left side. These facts are important in the understanding of the story.

The game of "chicken" is played when a driver keeps in the middle of the road all the time. Another driver, coming towards him, also keeps in the middle. The driver who leaves the middle, to avoid an accident, is the chicken. This dangerous game is played not only in America, but in other countries, and it has caused many unnecessary deaths.

CAN WE BE WARNED in a dream against a course of action which may be dangerous? I think this is hard to believe. If we can see the future in a dream (or otherwise), then surely the future already exists. If it does, then we have no freedom of action; we are not responsible for our own lives. How can our actions *matter* to ourselves or to anyone else?

Before I tell you the dream, I ought to explain a little. It was the summer of four years ago. I was driving my family back from Italy through the South of France. My son had not yet learned to drive. My daughter was too young to drive, and my wife doesn't drive. I had been driving for the best part of three weeks. Perhaps I was tired; perhaps I could think of nothing except cars. The town in which we spent this night of the dream was Tain l'Hermitage.

Now I'll tell you the dream. I was sitting in a big and powerful car. Its colour was cream. I was driving at high speed through the country. I was approaching a bend in the road, and in front of me there was an immense lorry.

My foot reached out towards the brake, but it did not touch anything. I looked down: there was no brake! Worse: my hands held empty air. There was no wheel for them to hold. There were no controls of any kind! Already we were almost into the back of the lorry.

I shouted in alarm. A calm voice came from my left side, and I turned my head. A stranger was sitting there. He was a cheerful man of middle age. He was wearing a silk shirt, and on his head he had a red cap. I couldn't understand what he said; he spoke in rapid French, and my own French is very poor. I didn't care what he said. My eyes were on his clean, fat hands, which held the steering-wheel. This car had the wheel on the left. He, not I, was in control.

We ran safely round the bend. He turned the steering-wheel slightly to place the car in the middle of the road. He was going to overtake the lorry. The road stretched straight ahead. It was bright in the sunlight and was quite empty. Only one other person was in sight. A woman was sitting outside a cottage which had white walls. This cottage was almost exactly ahead of us. She was sitting by a table and arranging some flowers. She wanted to sell some, and waved them towards us.

This sign, for some reason, filled me with a terrible fear. Then I noticed that the flowers were arranged in a circle. They were just like the flowers that we put on graves. They reminded me at once of death.

At this moment we were level with the lorry. In a few seconds we ought to have overtaken it; but then the lorry began to turn away from the side of the road, and towards our car. Its driver was doing this on purpose. The stranger by my side swore loudly and tried to turn away. There was a terrible noise of tearing from the back of the car, and then something exploded. The earth seemed to turn over, and the noise of flame roared in my ears. I awoke, and I was sweating.

I was very disturbed by this dream, and could not sleep again. It seemed to warn me about something, and I wanted to explain it.

Even if warnings are possible, this dream had no sense in it. What did it warn me against? Must I never overtake a lorry on a clear road? The road towards Paris is always filled with immense lorries. Most of them come up from Marseilles. I always have to pass them when the road is clear; I can't drive slowly behind them for ever. No. This was not the meaning of the dream. Its root was in some kind of fear. I must try to find the fear, and then I could forget it all.

I thought about my driving during the last three weeks. I tried to remember all the lorries and all the white cottages. I thought of all the cars which were painted cream. I remembered nothing of any great interest. I had supposed that the road in the dream must be in France; it was long, empty and straight. But then I remembered that we had overtaken the lorry on the right. So the dream was about a road in England. In England all cars keep to the left. Immediately I remembered something.

Two years before this, I had been travelling in the North of England. An American and I were preparing some programmes for the radio. He had brought his car from America, and of course its steering-wheel was on the left side. So were the brakes and other controls; but the colour of his car was not cream.

The American was a careless driver, and often overtook other cars against my advice. Remember that I was in a better position to see: I was sitting on the right. Once, beyond Nottingham, he played "chicken".

"Chicken", as you probably know, is a game on the roads. It is increasing in America, because long journeys can be very dull. You just move your car into the middle of the road and stay there. When another car appears, it comes towards you in the middle of the road. The driver who turns away is the chicken. Quite often neither turns away.

I gave him my ideas about this game in the strong language of the north of England. We did not play it again, but probably it had left its mark on my mind. So then, when I was asleep, I saw it all again in a dream. I also remembered another thing one day when I was having breakfast. When we played "chicken", it was an uncommonly windy day. We stopped at Chesterfield, and the American bought a cap. It was a black cap, not a red one; but in dreams details are not always exact.

After this I forgot the dream until the afternoon. The big French lorries often play their own game. They stay in the middle of the road, and you can't overtake. You have to stay behind them. Sometimes you have to follow them for endless miles, although the roads are otherwise empty.

This afternoon we were following an immense machine which was making terrible noises: perhaps it was loaded with big guns. When I blew my horn, the driver moved to the side of the road; but it was the wrong side. He drove along on the left, instead of keeping to the right. There was enough space on the right for me to pass him. But if I did that, I should be on the wrong side; so I just followed him for two miles. All the time I told myself not to overtake.

I considered the situation from every point of view. I could certainly turn my car more quickly than he could turn his lorry. It was a very big and heavy lorry. Could I, perhaps, pass him quickly before he could do anything? If he turned to the right, he could easily kill us all; and by law he ought to keep to the right. Probably he only wanted a bit of fun; but he *might* want an accident. If he killed us, nobody would know. Nobody could blame him; he would be in the right. But it was such a heavy lorry that I could probably pass safely. He would have no time to drive into us.

The road ahead was quite empty, and there were miles of it. I drove more slowly until some distance separated us. Then I increased my speed as much as I could. I drove towards that empty space beside the lorry. My car was moving at about seventy miles an hour.

The front of my car was almost level with the back of the lorry. Then I saw something that knocked the breath out of my body. A woman was sitting beside a table of flowers outside a white cottage! The table was standing on the grass beside the road.

For the first time in my life I changed my mind while I was overtaking. My foot went down hard on the brake. The car rocked and rolled. From behind I heard the sound of a horn. Another car was coming after us at a high speed. I knew its colour before I saw it; it was cream.

I pressed hard on the brake and turned the steering-wheel slightly. I was just able to get behind the lorry without touching it. The other car passed us and the driver blew his horn wildly. It reached the lorry – and then the lorry turned towards it.

For a moment I thought the car would pass the lorry safely; it was moving very fast. Then the front of the lorry just touched the back of the car. It was only a light touch but it knocked the car towards the side of the road. It ran fast towards the woman at the table.

The driver of that car was a master of the road. With the greatest skill he turned it back into the middle of the road.

My car was moving at about seventy miles an hour

If I had been in his place, I could not have done it. His control was wonderful. He waved angrily at the lorry driver, and drove rapidly away in a cloud of dust. He was soon out of sight.

We stayed that night in Fontainebleau. A big car was standing outside the hotel, and the back was newly scratched. Its colour was cream, and so I tried to find the driver. He was *not* wearing a red cap or a silk shirt.

He was a young man from Paris – not like the driver in my dream. He spoke good English; I asked him if he would like the number of that lorry. I had noticed it, and I could have given it to him. But he only laughed; the law won't help you if you overtake on the wrong side. He treated the whole thing as a game.

"It tests your skill," he said. "If the car is powerful enough, it can be done. But if *you* had tried, in your car, you would have failed."

I didn't tell him why I had hesitated. There was no time. He was in a hurry and wanted to reach Paris without delay. Let us suppose I had *not* hesitated. Well, . . . I don't really believe in dreams, of course; but something saved us all from a terrible death.

DARK THEY WERE WITH GOLDEN EYES
Ray Bradbury

Ray Douglas Bradbury was born in Illinois, U.S.A., in 1920, and married in 1947. Many of his short stories are based on science and the future of men.

His first stories appeared in various papers, and some of them were chosen for *Best American Short Stories*, 1946, 1948, and 1952. He has won several prizes with his books.

Among his best-known stories are *The Golden Apples of the Sun* (1953), *Fahrenheit 451* (1954), and *Something Wicked This Way Comes* (1963). He has also written one or two plays.

In *Dark They Were With Golden Eyes* he imagines a time in the future when travel to Mars is common. The Bittering family goes there so as to be safe from the atom bombs which will soon destroy the earth. Bittering himself at first plans to return to the earth later, but he never does.

When some later visitors from the earth reach Mars, they shout that they have won the war with their atom bombs. This piece of news, which appears very important to them, has little meaning in this other world. The new visitors immediately start to make plans to build cities like those on earth; but already one of the officers seems to be changing, as all visitors to Mars change in the end.

This short story is one of those included in *The Day It Rained Forever* (1959).

THE METAL of the rocket cooled in the winds. From it a man, a woman and three children stepped. The other travellers went off across the Martian field and left the man with his family.

The man felt his hair moving in the wind. His wife, in front of him, trembled. The children looked up at him. His face was cold.

"What's wrong?" his wife asked.

"Let us get back to the rocket," he said.

"And go back to Earth?"

"Yes! Listen!"

The wind was blowing. At any moment the air of Mars could draw his soul out of him. He looked at the Martian hills, which time had worn away. They had been changed by the years. He saw the old cities. They were lost and dying in the grass, like the delicate bones of children.

"Cheer up, Harry!" his wife said. "It's too late to go back. We've come sixty-five million miles, at least."

The children with their yellow hair shouted at the Martian sky. There was no answer except the rush of the wind through the stiff grass.

He picked up the bags in his cold hands. "Come along," he said. He was a man who was standing on the edge of something new. He was like a man by the sea. He was ready to walk into it and be drowned.

They walked into the town.

Their name was Bittering: Harry Bittering and his wife, Cora. Tim, Laura and David were the children. They built a small white cottage and ate good breakfasts there. But the fear was always with them. It went to bed with them; it was at every talk in the evenings; it was with them when morning came.

"We don't belong here," he often said. "We're the people of Earth. This is Mars. This place was intended for Martians. Let us buy tickets for home, Cora, please!"

She only shook her head. "One day the atom bomb will kill everyone on Earth," she said. "When that happens, we'll be safe here."

"Safe and mad!" he said.

"But there aren't any atom bombs on Mars," she said.

The voice-clock spoke: *Time to get up!* it said. *Seven o'clock.* So they got up.

Something made him examine everything each morning. He expected that he might find something wrong. The morning paper came regularly on the rocket from Earth. It arrived at six o'clock. He opened it at breakfast and spoke cheerfully.

"In another year, there'll be a million men on Mars!" he said. "A million men from Earth! Big cities here! They said we should fail. They said the Martians wouldn't like us here. But did we find any Martians? Not one! Oh, we found empty cities, but there was nobody in them. Am I right?"

A great wind shook the house. When the windows were quiet again, Mr. Bittering looked at the children.

"I don't know," David said. "Perhaps there are some Martians that we don't see. Sometimes I think I hear them at night. I hear the wind, and the sand hits my window. I'm frightened. I see those towns on the mountains where the Martians lived. But that was a long time ago, wasn't it? I think I see things in the towns. The things move round the towns, Father! And I wonder about the Martians. Do they *like* us here? Perhaps they'll do something to us because we came here."

"Nonsense!" Mr. Bittering looked out of the window. "We're clean, good people." He looked at his children. "All dead cities have something strange in them – spirits, memories!" He looked at the hills. "Perhaps sometimes you see some stairs. You wonder who went up them. What did the Martians look like when they were climbing those stairs? Then perhaps you see some Martian pictures. You wonder who painted them. What was he like? You imagine things." He stopped. "You haven't been up in those ruins, have you?"

"No, Father." David looked down at his shoes.

"Stay away from them and pass the butter."

"But something will happen," little David said.

Something happened that afternoon. Laura ran through the

little town, and she was crying.

"Mother! Father! The war! Earth! A radio flash has just come! Atom bombs have hit New York! All the rockets have exploded! There won't be any more rockets to Mars, ever!"

"Oh, Harry!" The mother held the arms of her husband and daughter.

"Are you sure, Laura?" asked the father quietly.

"We're prisoners on Mars for ever," said Laura with tears.

For a long time there was only the sound of the wind in the late afternoon.

"We're alone!" Bittering thought. "Only a thousand of us here. There's no way back: no way." Sweat poured from his face and hands and body. He wanted to strike Laura. He wanted to say, "You're lying! The rockets *will* come back." Instead, he said gently, "The rockets will come one day!"

"In five years, perhaps," she said. "It takes five years to build a rocket. What shall we do, Father? What shall we do?"

"Do our work, of course. Grow the crops. Go on until the war ends. Then the rockets will come again."

The two boys came. "Children," he said, "I want to tell you something."

"We know," they said.

Bittering wandered into the garden to stand alone in his fear. While the rockets regularly crossed space, he had been able to accept Mars. He had always told himself, "Tomorrow, if I want, I can buy a ticket. I can go back to Earth."

But now the rockets were old metal. The people of Earth were left to the strangeness of Mars. They had only the strange dust, the strange air. They had the hot Martian summers, and the cold, cold winters. What was going to happen to him and the others? Mars had been waiting for this moment. Now Mars was going to eat them.

He got down on his knees among the flowers. He took a spade in his weak hands. "Work!" he thought. "Work and forget!"

He looked up from the garden towards the Martian mountains. He thought of their proud Martian names in the

Atom bombs have hit New York

older days. Men had come from Earth to the Martian sky. They had dropped down and looked at Martian seas and rivers. Once the Martians had built cities and had given them names. They had climbed mountains and named them. They had sailed seas and named the seas. Then mountains and seas changed, and cities fell to ruin. The men from Earth had given new names to these ancient hills and valleys; but they had felt guilty about it.

Mr. Bittering felt very alone in his garden under the Martian sun. He bent down and planted Earth flowers in the Martian soil.

He talked to himself. "Think!" he said. "Think of different things. Keep your mind free from thoughts of Earth. Forget the rockets. Forget the atom bombs."

He sweated and took his coat off. He hung it on a tree which had come from Massachusetts.

He thought about the names again. The men from Earth had given these names. There were Ford Hills and a Roosevelt Sea on Mars. It wasn't right! People who had settled in America in the old days had used the old names: Wisconsin, Minnesota, Idaho, Ohio, Utah. These were old Indian names with old meanings.

He looked wildly up at the mountains and thought, "Are you up there? You Martians, dead Martians, are you all there? Well, here we are, alone! We're separated from Earth now. Come down and move us out of your Mars. If you do that, we can't do anything."

The wind blew some blossoms along. He put out a brown hand and gave a cry. He touched the blossoms and picked them up. He turned them over, and touched them again and again. Then he called to his wife.

"Cora!"

She appeared at a window. He ran to her.

"Cora, look at these blossoms!"

She touched them.

"Do you see?" he asked. "They're different! They've changed! They're not the same as before."

"They look all right to me," she said.

"They're not! They're *wrong*. I don't know what it is. An extra leaf, perhaps. Or perhaps it's the colour or the smell."

The children ran out and saw their father. He was hurrying round the garden. He was pulling plants up to look at them.

"Cora, come and look!"

They touched the plants. "Do they look right?" he asked. "Are they the same as they were before?"

She hesitated. "I don't know," she said.

"They've changed," he said.

"Perhaps."

"You know they have! The smell isn't the same now." His heart was beating heavily, and he was afraid. He dug his fingers into the soil. "Cora, what's happening? What is it? We must get away from this." He ran across the garden. Each tree felt his touch. "The roses! The roses!" he cried. "Look at them. The roses are turning green!"

They stood and looked at the green roses.

Two days later Tim ran into the house. "Come and see the cow," he cried. "I saw it. Come and look!"

They went out and looked at their one cow. It was growing a third horn. And the grass in front of their house was quietly changing its colour. Slowly it was turning to a soft purple.

"We must get away!" Bittering said. "If we eat this stuff, we'll change too. What shall we change into? I can't let it happen. We must burn this food. That's the only thing we can do."

"It's not poisoned," she said.

"But it is. It's secretly poisoned. We mustn't touch it."

He looked anxiously at the house. "Even the house has changed," he said. "The wind's done something to it. The air's burned it. The boards are all out of shape. It's not a house for a man from Earth any more."

"Oh, you're imagining things!"

He put his coat on. "I'm going into town. I have some work to do. I'll be back soon."

"Wait, Harry!" his wife cried.

But he had gone.

In the town the men sat with their hands on their knees. They were talking calmly on the steps of the shop.

Mr. Bittering wanted to fire a gun. "What are you doing, you fools?" he thought. "You've heard the news. We're prisoners on this planet, and you're just sitting there. Aren't you frightened? Aren't you afraid? What are you going to do?"

"Hullo, Harry," everyone said.

"Listen," he said. "You did hear the news, didn't you?"

They laughed. "Sure, Harry," they said. "Of course!"

"What are you going to do about it?" he asked. "How are you going to get away from this planet?"

"What *can* we do?" they said.

"We can build a rocket," he said.

"A rocket, Harry? Why? To go back to all that trouble? Oh, Harry!"

"But you *must* want to go back. Have you noticed the blossoms and the colour of the grass?"

"Yes, we have, Harry," one of the men said.

"Don't they frighten you?"

"I don't remember that they frightened us much, Harry."

"Fools!"

"Oh, Harry! Don't talk like that."

Bittering wanted to cry. "You've got to work with me. If we stay here, we'll all change. Don't you smell the air? There's something in the air. There's something Martian in it. Listen to me!"

They just looked at him.

"Sam!" he said to one of them.

"Yes, Harry?"

"Will you help me to build a rocket?"

"I've got a lot of metal, Harry. If you want to work in my factory, you're welcome. I'll sell you that metal for five hundred dollars. You ought to be able to build a fine rocket. If you work alone, you can finish it in about thirty years. Then you can leave our planet."

Everyone laughed.

"Don't laugh!" Bittering said.

Sam looked at him quietly.

"Sam," Bittering said, "your eyes . . ." He paused. "They were grey eyes, weren't they?"

"Well, I don't remember," Sam said. "Why do you ask, Harry?"

"Because now they're yellow."

"Is that so, Harry?" Sam said carelessly.

"And you're taller and thinner."

"You may be right, Harry."

"Sam, you ought not to have yellow eyes."

"Harry, what colour are your own eyes?"

"My eyes?" Bittering said. "They're blue, of course."

"Here you are, Harry," Sam said. He gave him a small mirror. "Take a look at yourself."

Mr. Bittering hesitated, and then raised the mirror to his face. In the blue of his eyes he saw little bits of gold. The mirror fell down.

"Now you've broken my mirror!" Sam cried.

Harry Bittering began to build the rocket in Sam's factory. Men stood in the open door and joked quietly. Sometimes they helped him to lift something; but usually they just watched him with their yellow eyes.

His wife brought him his supper in a basket. "I won't eat it," he said. "I'll eat nothing from our garden. I'll only eat the food from Earth: the food that's frozen."

His wife stood and watched. "You can't build a rocket, Harry," she said.

"I worked with metal when I was twenty," he said. "When I've started properly, the others'll help." He did not look at her. "We've got to get away from this planet, Cora!" he said.

The nights were full of wind that crossed the empty fields. The moon shone on little white cities that were twelve thousand years old. Bittering's house shook with a feeling of change.

The moon shone on little white cities

In bed Mr. Bittering knew that his bones were changing and melting. His wife was dark from many afternoons in the sun. Dark she was, and golden. The children were like metal in their beds. The sad wind roared through the old trees and the purple grass. The fear did not end. It held his heart and throat. She was golden now! A green star rose in the east. It was another planet: his old planet, Earth.

A strange word came from Mr. Bittering's lips: "*Iorrt. Iorrt.*" He repeated it: "*Iorrt.*"

It was a Martian word, but he knew no Martian.

In the middle of the night he arose and telephoned to Simpson. Simpson knew a lot about the past.

"Simpson, what does the word *Iorrt* mean?" Bittering said.

"Oh, that's the old Martian word for our planet, Earth. Why?"

"No special reason," Bittering said.

The telephone slipped from his hand. "Hullo! Hullo! Hullo!" it called again and again. He sat and looked at the green star. "Bittering!" the telephone called. "Harry! Are you there?"

The days were full of the sound of metal. He began to build the frame of the rocket, and three men helped him. After an hour's work he was very tired, and had to sit down.

"Are you *eating*, Harry?" one of them asked.

"I'm eating," he replied angrily.

"From the food of Earth?"

"Yes."

"You're getting thinner, Harry."

"I'm not!"

"And taller!"

"Lies!" he shouted.

His wife spoke serious!y to him a few days later. "Harry, I've used up all the food from Earth. Nothing's left. I'll have to give you food which is grown on Mars."

He sat down heavily. "On Mars!" he said. "Near the green roses!"

"You must eat," she said. "You're getting weak."

"Yes," he said.

He began to eat something. "And take a holiday today," she said. "The children want to swim in the canals. Please come with us."

"I mustn't waste time!" he cried.

"Come just for an hour," she begged. "You'll feel better after a swim."

He stood up, hot. "Well," he said, "I'll come."

"Good!"

The sun was hot and the day was quiet. The sun was burning the land. The father, the mother and the children moved along the canal. Then they stopped to eat something. He noticed their skins. They were getting browner. He saw the yellow eyes of his wife and children. Their eyes had never been yellow before – never golden before. He was almost afraid again, but he was too tired to be afraid. He lay in the warm sun.

"Cora, how long have your eyes been yellow?"

She hesitated. "Always, I suppose."

"Didn't they change from brown in the last three months?"

She bit her lips. "No. Why do you ask?"

"Never mind," he said. "The children's eyes too; they're yellow."

"Sometimes children's eyes change colour when the children are growing."

"Perhaps *we're* children too," he said. "Children here on Mars. That's a thought." He laughed and jumped into the water. At the bottom, all was quiet and peaceful.

"If I lay here long enough," he thought, "the water would eat away my flesh. It would leave the bones and nothing else. Then things from the water would grow on the bones. Change! Change! Slow and silent change!"

He came up and saw Tim. The boy was sitting on the bank of the canal.

"*Utha*," Tim said.

"What?" his father asked.

The boy smiled. "You know," he said. "*Utha* is the Martian word for *Father*."

"Where did you learn it?"

"I don't know. Around here. *Utha!*"

"What do you want?"

The boy hesitated. "I – I want to change my name."

"Change it?"

"Yes."

His mother came. "What's wrong with *Tim?*" she asked. "It's a good name." She looked at the water. It was like a glass mirror.

"Once you called *Tim, Tim,*" the boy said. "I didn't even hear. I said to myself, 'That's not my name. I've a new name and I want to use it'."

Mr. Bittering held the side of the canal, and his heart beat heavily. "What's the new name?" he asked.

"*Linnl*. Isn't that a good name? I'm *Linnl*. Can I use that name please?"

Mr. Bittering put his hand to his head. He thought of the rocket and he thought of himself. He was always alone. He worked alone on the rocket, and he was alone even among his family.

He heard his wife saying, "Why not?"

He heard himself saying, "Yes, you can use it."

The boy shouted with joy. "I'm Linnl!" he cried. "Linnl!" He ran through the fields and danced. "Linnl!" he shouted.

Mr. Bittering looked at his wife. "Why did we do that?" he asked.

"I don't know," she said. "It seemed to be a good idea."

They walked into the hills. They went along old paths and beside old fountains. The paths were covered with cool water during the whole of the summer. They kept bare feet cool.

They reached an empty Martian villa. It had a good view of the valley; it stood on the top of a hill. It had halls which were made of blue stone. There was a pool for swimming. It refreshed them on this hot summer day. The Martians hadn't liked large cities.

"We ought to live up here in a villa during the summer," Mrs. Bittering said.

"Come on," he said. "We're going back to the town. I have to work on the rocket."

While he was working that night, he remembered the blue villa. As the hours passed, the rocket seemed less important. Days and weeks passed, and the rocket was almost forgotten. The old fever had gone; but he was frightened when he remembered.

One hot day he heard the men talking. "Everyone's going," they were saying.

Bittering came out. "Where?" he said. He saw two cars filled with children. He saw two lorries which were full of furniture.

"Up to the mountains," they said. "To the cool villas. Are you coming, Harry?"

"I've got to work here," he said.

"Work? You can finish the rocket in the autumn, when it's cooler." Their voices were lazy in the heat.

"I've got to work," he repeated.

"Autumn!" they said. They seemed to speak with reason and sense. They seemed so right.

"There's plenty of time in the autumn," he thought. But part of him cried, "No, no!"

"In the autumn," he said. "Yes! I'll begin work again in the autumn."

"I've got a villa near the Tirra Canal," one of them said.

"You mean the Roosevelt Canal, don't you?"

"Tirra Canal! It's the old Martian name."

"But on the map . . ." Bittering began.

"Forget the map. It's the Tirra Canal now. I've found a villa in the Pillan Mountains."

"You mean the Rockefeller Mountains," Bittering said.

"I mean the Pillan Mountains," Sam said.

"Yes," said Bittering to the hot air. "Yes. The Pillan

Mountains."

Everyone helped to load the lorry in the hot afternoon of the next day. Laura, Tim and David carried packets. But they preferred the Martian names: Ttil, Linnl and Werr carried packets. The furniture was left in the little white cottage. "It looked fine in Boston," the mother said. "And it looked good here in the cottage. But it doesn't suit a villa. We'll get it when we come back in the autumn."

"I'm going to be lazy at the villa," Bittering said.

"Are you going to take your New York dresses," they asked the daughter.

The girl was puzzled by the question. "Oh!" she cried. "I don't want those things any longer!"

They locked the doors of the cottage and the father looked into the lorry. "We're not taking much, are we?" he cried. "We brought a lot of things to Mars, but we haven't got much here."

He started the engine, and looked back at the small cottage. For a long moment he wanted to rush to it. He wanted to say good-bye to it. He felt that they were going away on a long journey. It seemed that they would never return to the old life. They were leaving it now, perhaps for ever.

Just then Sam and his family drove past in another lorry. Sam called out, "Hullo, Bittering! Here we go!"

Sixty other lorries were travelling along the same old road. When they left the town, it was filled with heavy dust. The water of the canal looked blue in the sunlight. A quiet wind moved in the strange trees.

"Good-bye, town!" said Mr. Bittering.

"Good-bye, good-bye!" cried the family. They waved their hands to it and did not look back again.

Summer burned the canals and they dried up. Summer moved across the fields like flame. In the empty town of the Earth people the paint came off the houses. The frame of the rocket began to look old. Bits of it started to fall off.

In the quiet autumn Mr. Bittering stood on the slope above

his villa. He was very dark now, and his eyes were golden. He looked at the valley.

"We ought to go back," Cora said. "The time has come."

"Yes," he said; "but we're not going. There's nothing there now."

"Your books," she said, "and your fine clothes."

"The town's empty," he said. "Nobody's going back. There's no reason now."

The daughter sewed, and the sons played songs on old instruments. The sound of their laughing filled the beautiful villa. Mr. Bittering looked at the old town far away in the valley. "The Earth people built very foolish houses," he said.

"They didn't know any better way," she said. "I'm glad they've gone. They were ugly people."

They both looked at each other and were surprised. They laughed.

"Where did they go?" he wondered. He looked for a moment at his wife. She was golden like his daughter. She looked at him; he seemed almost as young as their eldest son.

"I don't know where they went," she said.

"We'll go back to the town next year, perhaps," he said. "Or the year after, or the year after that. Now – I'm warm. Shall we take a swim?"

They turned their backs to the valley. Arm in arm they walked silently along a path. It was covered with clear water.

Five years later a rocket fell out of the sky. It lay in the valley, and men jumped out of it. They were shouting.

"We won the war on Earth! We've come to rescue you! Where are you?"

But the town of the Earth people was silent. The cottages, the old trees and the theatre were silent. The Americans found the frame of a rocket. It was not complete, and it looked old.

The men from the rocket searched the hills. The captain set up his office in an old house. One of the officers soon returned to report to him.

"The town's empty, sir; but we found some Martian life in

the hills. They're dark people with yellow eyes. They don't want any quarrels. They learn English fast, and we talked a bit. We shan't have to fight them, sir."

"Dark?" the captain said thoughtfully. "How many?"

"Six or eight hundred. They're living in those old villas in the hills. They're tall and strong. Their women are very beautiful."

"Did they tell you what happened to the Earth people? Where are the people who built this town here?"

"They don't know a thing about the town, sir."

"That's strange," the captain said. "Do you think the Martians killed the Earth people?"

"They seem very peaceful, sir. Perhaps some kind of sickness killed this town."

"Perhaps! I suppose we'll never know the truth."

The captain looked round the room with its dusty windows. He saw the blue mountains far away, and the water in the canals. He heard the soft wind and trembled a little. Then he put his finger on a map on the table.

"We've got a lot of work to do," he said. His voice continued quietly while the sun sank behind the blue hills. "We have to make some new towns. We must find the right places for the mines. The old records have all been lost. New maps must be made, and new names must be given to the mountains. We must find names for the rivers too."

The other officer was silent, and so he continued. "What do you think of *Lincoln Mountains* and *Washington Canal*? Give me some more names. We can call this place *Einstein Valley*, can't we? And there . . . Are you *listening* to me?"

The other officer pulled his eyes away from the blue colour and the quiet mist of the distant hills.

"What? Oh, *yes*, sir."

IT HAPPENED NEAR A LAKE
John Collier

John Henry Noyes Collier was born in 1901 at Carshalton, and was privately educated. His books include *Tom's A-cold* (1933) and several other full-length stories; he has also written short stories and poems. He is fond of gardening, and now lives in the U.S.A.

In this story Mr. Beaseley is a shopkeeper who has never made much money or done anything unusual or interesting. His wife treats him badly, and he tries to escape from his dull life by reading about the wonders of science. One day he receives a large number of dollars and decides to travel to interesting places. The first place he chooses is Yucatan. (Yucatan is mostly in Mexico; its famous ruins are chiefly those of splendid buildings put up by men of an ancient civilization.) His wife wants to have a flat in New York and a house in Miami; but she does not want him to escape from her, and so she travels with him (angrily). She behaves unpleasantly everywhere. When they go up the River Amazon in search of a terrible creature in a lake, she at last loses all patience. She declares that she will leave for Para. (This is a port at the mouth of the Amazon; its full name is Belem do Para.) In fact, she never leaves the lake, and the story explains why.

Mr. Beaseley was fifty. He was shaving and he was looking at his face in the glass. It showed him that he was very like a mouse.

"I'm older," he thought. "But what do I care? I don't care, except for Maria. And how old she's getting, too!"

He finished his dressing and hurried down the stairs. He thought anxiously that he was probably late for breakfast. Immediately after breakfast, he had to open his shop; and that always kept him busy until ten o'clock at night. He never made much money although he worked so long. Sometimes during the day Maria came into the shop and showed him his mistakes. She did this even when there were people there.

He found a little comfort every morning when he opened the newspaper. When he read it, he could escape from his dull life. For a short time he could forget it. On Fridays he enjoyed himself more than on other days. On Fridays he received his copy of the other paper, *Wonders of Science*. This paper showed him one way out of his terrible and hopeless life. With *Wonders of Science* he escaped from the dull house into a splendid country.

On this particular morning, splendid news kindly came to Mr. Beaseley in his own home. It came on fine paper in a long envelope from a lawyer.

"Believe it or not, my dear," Mr. Beaseley said to his wife. "Someone has died. I've been left four hundred thousand dollars."

"What?" she said. "Where? Let me see! Don't keep the letter to yourself like that! Give it to me!"

"Go on!" said he. "Read it! Push your nose into it! Do you think it will help you?"

"Oh!" she cried. "The money has made you rude already!"

"Yes," he said thoughtfully. "I've been left four hundred thousand dollars. Four hundred thousand!"

"We'll be able to have a flat in New York," she said, "or a little house in Miami."

"You may have half the money," said Mr. Beaseley. "You

may do as you like with it. I myself intend to travel."

Mrs. Beaseley heard this remark without pleasure. He belonged to her. She never liked losing anything that belonged to her. She always wanted to keep everything, even old and useless things.

"So you want to leave me!" she cried.

"I want to see other places, unusual places, different places. In *Wonders of Science* it says that some people have very long necks. I want to see them. And I want to see the very little people, and some of the strange birds. I want to go to Yucatan. I have offered you half the money because you like city life. You like high society, but I prefer to travel. If you want to come with me, come."

She did not hesitate much. "I will," she said. "And don't forget I'm doing it for your sake. I have to keep you on the right path. When you're tired of wandering about with your mouth open, we'll buy a house. We'll have a flat in New York and a house in Miami."

So Mrs. Beaseley went angrily with him. She hated it; but she was ready to bear anything that took away some happiness from her husband. Their journeys took them into deep forests. Their bedroom walls and floors were often made of bare wood; but outside the window there was a beautiful scene like a painting. The colours of the flowers and the straightness of the trees looked fine in the bright light.

In the high Andes their window was a square of burning blue. Sometimes a small white cloud appeared in a lower corner of the square. On islands in the sun they took huts by the sea. There the tide brought offerings to their door in the mornings. They found shells on the sand or creatures of the sea. Mr. Beaseley was glad, but his wife preferred bottles of wine to shells. She dreamed every day of a flat in New York; or she thought of a little house in Miami. She tried endlessly to punish the man because he kept them from her.

When a beautiful bird settled on a branch over her husband's head, she gave a terrible cry. Then the bird flew away before

Mr. Beaseley had the time to examine it. He wanted to see birds like that, but she tried to prevent him. They planned a trip to some old buildings in Yucatan; but she told him the wrong time for the start of the journey. When he tried to watch an interesting animal, she pretended to have something in her eye. So he had to look into it and get the thing out. Usually he found nothing.

She was determined to stay in Buenos Aires for a long time. Her hair had to be arranged; she needed a permanent wave. She also needed some better clothes, and she wanted to go to the races. Mr. Beaseley agreed because he wanted to be just.

They took rooms in a comfortable hotel. One day, when his wife was at the races, Mr. Beaseley met a little Portuguese doctor. Soon they were talking happily together. They discussed some of the strange creatures which lived in South America.

"I have recently returned from the River Amazon," said the doctor. "The lakes are terrible. In one of them there is a very strange creature. Science knows nothing about it, but the Indians have seen it. It is immensely big. It lives in the water and has a very long neck. Its teeth are like swords."

Mr. Beaseley was delighted. "What a monster!" he cried happily.

"Yes, yes," said the Portuguese doctor. "It is certainly interesting."

"I must go there!" cried Mr. Beaseley. "I must talk to those Indians. If there's a monster in the lake, I must see it. Will you show me the way? Are you free just now? Can you come with me?"

The doctor agreed, and everything was arranged without delay. Mrs. Beaseley returned from the races and learnt of the new plan without much joy. She was told that they were going to start almost immediately. The two men explained that they would live near the unknown lake. They would spend their time among the Indians.

She was not pleased, and she insulted the little doctor. He

Soon they were talking happily together

only gave a polite reply to her hard words. He had no need to worry. He was going to be paid highly for his help.

Mrs. Beaseley complained loudly all the way up the river. She told her husband that there was no monster in the lake. She mentioned that the doctor was not an honest man. Although her husband often suffered from this kind of remark, he was hurt. He felt ashamed in front of the Portuguese. His wife's voice, too, was loud and sharp. One result was that every animal hurried away from them. Mr. Beaseley saw nothing of the animals except their back legs. They all left the great river and the terrible voice at high speed. They hid themselves in the dark forest behind the biggest trees.

The little party reached the lake after many days on the river.

"How do we know that this is the right place?" Mrs. Beaseley said to her husband. She was watching the doctor, who was talking to some Indians. "It is probably any lake. It's not a special one. What are those Indians saying to him? You can't understand a word. You're ready to believe anything, aren't you? You'll never see the monster. Only a fool would believe that story."

Mr. Beaseley gave no reply. The doctor continued his conversation with the Indians, and they gave him some useful news. They told him about a hut which was made of grass. It was near the lake and no one was using it. The little party found this hut after great efforts, and they stayed in it for several days. Mr. Beaseley watched the lake every day, but never saw the monster. In fact, he saw nothing at all. Mrs. Beaseley was very satisfied with this result of their long journey, but she always looked angry.

One day she spoke severely to her husband. "I will bear this kind of life no longer," she said. "I've allowed you to drag me from one place to another. I've tried to watch you and take care of you all the time. I've travelled hundreds of miles in an open boat with Indians. Now you're wasting your money on a man who only wants to trick you. We shall leave for Para in the morning."

"You may go if you wish," said he. "I'll write you a cheque for two hundred thousand dollars. Perhaps you can persuade an Indian to take you down the river in a boat. But I will not come with you."

"We shall see," she said. She had no wish to leave her husband alone. She was afraid that he might enjoy himself.

He wrote out the cheque and gave it to her. She still threatened to leave him, but she stayed.

She got up early the next morning and went outside the hut. She decided to have breakfast alone, and walked angrily towards some trees. It was her intention to get some fruit from the trees; but she had not gone far when she noticed a mark on the sand. It was the mark of an immense foot nearly a yard wide. The toes seemed to have sharp nails, and the next footprint was ten feet away.

Mrs. Beaseley looked without interest at the marks which the monster had left. No very strong feelings reached her mind. She was only angry at the thought of her husband's success. She was angry because the Portuguese had been telling the truth. She neither cried out in wonder, nor called to the sleeping men. She only gave a kind of bitter laugh.

Then she picked up a small branch which was lying on the ground. The monster's footprints had never been seen before by a European, but she rubbed it out with the branch. When this had been done thoroughly, she smiled bitterly. There was now no sign of the mark, and so she looked for the next one. She wiped that mark off the sand too. Further on she saw another, and then one more. She rubbed both out. Then she saw another, moved towards it, and rubbed it out. She continued in this way, holding the branch with both hands. In a short time she had rubbed out every mark down to the edge of the lake. The last footprint was partly in the water. The monster had clearly gone back to the lake.

Mrs. Beaseley rubbed out the last mark with pleasure, and then stood up straight. She looked back sourly towards the hut.

Mrs Beaseley rubbed out the last mark

She said some words to her husband, who was asleep up there. "I will tell you about this," she said, "when we are far away. We shall be living at Miami, and you will be an old man. You will never have seen the footprint or the monster. You'll be too old to do anything then."

At that moment there was a sound in the water behind her. She was seized by a set of teeth. The Portuguese doctor had described these teeth very well: they were exactly like swords. He had mentioned various other details, but she had no time to prove their correctness. After she had given one short cry, she was pulled under the water. Her cry was not heard by either of the men. It was given in a weak voice. She had used her voice too much during the past weeks, and it was tired.

A short time later Mr. Beaseley awoke. He saw that his wife was absent. He went to talk to the doctor, and mentioned the fact; but the doctor knew nothing and went to sleep again. Mr. Beaseley went outside and looked round for his wife; but he could see nothing. He returned to his friend.

"I think my wife has run away," he explained. "I've found her footprints. They lead down to the lake. I suppose she saw an Indian in his boat. Perhaps he has taken her away from here. She was threatening to leave yesterday. She wants to take a small house in Miami."

"That is not a bad place," the doctor replied; "but probably Buenos Aires is a better one. This monster is a great disappointment, my dear friend. Let us go back to Buenos Aires. I will show you some things there that will surprise you. They are very different from anything here, of course."

"You're a very good companion," said Mr. Beaseley. "You make even life in a city seem attractive."

"If you get tired of it," the Portuguese said, "we can always move on. I know some wonderful islands, and they have splendid people in them. We can visit them after we leave the cities."

THE UGLY AMERICAN AND THE UGLY SARKHANESE
W. J. Lederer and E. Burdick

This short story is taken from *The Ugly American,* a book which first appeared in 1959. It is not a true story, but the writers have travelled widely in Asia and they know the place and its people. Sarkhan is not a real country, but it represents the countries of that part of the world.

These American writers are not satisfied with the work that America is doing in the world. To them it appears to be badly planned. Where a pump is needed, America builds immense water-works. She builds fine long roads through forests, even when there are no cars to use them. She ought to plan more simply. This is one of the writers' ideas.

Another is that men who go to a foreign country ought to learn its language. In this story, the reader will notice that this point is also made. The headman is glad when Homer Atkins speaks to him in his own language. Atkins succeeds in his plan because he speaks the language; because he does not stay in the chief cities; because he knows what the people really need; and because he works with his hands and lives among the people.

This is the message which the writers give us in the book. It is a message of criticism, but they agree that there are many fine Americans abroad, doing good work. They want the work to be better, and the world to be a happier place as a result.

HOMER ATKINS looked angrily round the room. The other men sat there in their beautiful clothes and returned his look with bitterness. He was the only man without a tie, and the only engineer there. One of the others was the ambassador. Atkins wanted to tell them all that they were fools; but it is not easy to tell an ambassador that he is a fool. The others, too, were important in their different governments. So he did not say it.

"I was asked to come here, gentlemen," he said, "to give advice. I build roads and move earth. That's my work. You say that you want roads; but I tell you that you don't need any. I've been here ten months, and I've walked all over the country. I've talked to a thousand people, and I've sent in my report."

"But Mr. Atkins," said one of the smooth gentlemen, "you haven't told us much about the roads. Where ought they to go?"

"You don't need any. You need things that the people here can make: small things, but useful things. What do the people care about roads for the army? Here you can think of nothing else: roads, and only roads. But go out into the country, and take a look there. You've got some good people away out there. Build some factories for them. Let them make tins and put food in them. Forget the roads until you've got more money."

"Mr. Atkins, this is not your business. You've been asked where the roads ought to be put. No one has asked you whether you prefer roads or factories. You must leave that sort of decision to others. They must decide, not you."

"Who ought to decide? People like you? Which of you has been out into the country? What do you know about the villages?"

There was a silence.

"Which of you has been out into the country?" Atkins asked again. The silence remained unbroken. There were many red faces in the room.

"Build a factory to make bricks," Atkins said. "Let some of the people get stone out of the ground too. There's a lot of very fine stone out there. It can be used for building. And make use of that good soil near the coast."

"That's the work of the agricultural men," someone said. "You know nothing about soil. You're a man who builds roads."

"Very well!" Atkins said. He got up and walked out of the room; but the ambassador went out too and followed him.

"Come and have a drink," the ambassador said. "I like the things that you say."

"No one else likes them," said Atkins with a bitter laugh.

"Mr. Atkins," the ambassador said, "are you willing to go to Sarkhan?"

"Why? Have you any problems there?"

They were sitting together with their drinks. "Sarkhan is a country which has a lot of hills," the ambassador said. "Crops are grown on terraces on the hills. They have to work hard when they raise water from the rivers below. The fields above need the water, but it is slow work. Can you help us on that problem? Can you find an easy way of raising water to the terraces?"

"Perhaps! Perhaps!" Atkins took a pencil and began to draw. "You need a simple pump," he said. He was busy for fifteen minutes and did not speak.

"Well, it may be interesting," he said then. "Yes, it may be quite interesting."

Two weeks later Atkins and his wife flew to Sarkhan. His wife, Emma, was almost as ugly as her husband. They went to live in a small cottage near Haidho.

The floors of the house were made of earth; they had one tap for water. There were thousands of insects, and one Sarkhanese boy. He was nine, and had dark eyes; his name was Ong. He appeared at six o'clock every morning and stayed all day.

Emma Atkins enjoyed herself in Sarkhan. She liked working in her house and she kept it well. It was as good as the houses of her neighbours.

Homer Atkins was busy with his pump. It was a pump for

water, and it had to be driven by hand. The idea developed very slowly in his mind. The people needed good pumps to raise water. They used buckets to do this, but the work was hard and slow. One man lifted the bucket to the terrace, and another man emptied it there. The Sarkhanese had been doing this for many years, and they did not like the thought of change. There seemed to be no reason for change; but Atkins knew that he must find a better way of moving the water. Talking was useless. He had to do something to help.

A simple pump needed three things. First it had to have cheap pipes. This was not a difficult problem. He had decided that the pipes could be made of bamboo. There was plenty of bamboo in the place. Secondly, the pump itself had to be made, and this problem was also solved. Outside many Sarkhanese villages there were the wrecks of old jeeps which the army had thrown away. Atkins had taken a piston from one of these jeeps for his pump. He had also cut one of the cylinders out of the engine of the jeep. He was able to arrange the piston and the cylinder together. The piston sucked the water up very well; it could raise the water thirty feet.

The third problem had not been solved. It was to find something to drive the pump.

He talked to his wife about this problem. "It must be something that can be found here in Sarkhan," he explained. "I don't want to bring something from abroad. If I did that, it would cost too much; and perhaps the Sarkhanese wouldn't understand it. Most of the farmers haven't been abroad."

"Why don't you give these nice people some good engines?" Emma asked. "You've got all that money in the bank at Pittsburg. You're rich enough."

"You know the reason," he said. "When you give a man something for nothing, he doesn't like you. You're the first man that he hates. If this pump is going to work properly, it must be a Sarkhanese pump. If I gave them part of it, it would be my pump."

Emma smiled fondly at Homer. She turned and looked out

of the window. She saw a group of Sarkhanese on bicycles; they were riding as usual towards the markets of Haidho. She watched them for a few moments. Then she turned round suddenly, and her eyes were excited.

"Why don't you use bicycles?" she asked. "There are millions of them in this country, and they must break down sometimes. Couldn't you use part of an old bicycle to drive each pump?"

Atkins looked at Emma's face and slowly sat up straight.

"I believe you've found the answer, old girl," he said softly. "We can take the wheels off an old bicycle. We can use the chain to drive the piston up and down in the cylinder. I can fix that. Yes! That can be done." He began to walk round the room. Emma, with a little smile, returned to her cooking. In a few moments she heard the sound of papers; she knew that her Homer was drawing something. Two hours later he was still drawing. An hour after that he started to drink beer. When the time came for dinner, he had drunk a lot of beer: about six bottles.

"I think I've found the answer," he said. He began to explain the machine to her. She made him sit down and eat his dinner; but he ate very fast and talked about his drawings all the time. Emma watched her husband fondly. She was proud of him. She was happy when he was happy. Today she felt very happy indeed.

"Stop drinking beer, Homer," she said. "And don't forget that it was my idea about the bicycle."

"Your idea?" he shouted. "Woman, you're mad. I was thinking about it all the time. You just reminded me of it."

Two days later he had a model of the machine. Every part of it could be found in the country; nothing needed to be brought from anywhere else. There were probably enough old bicycles to make two thousand pumps; but first he had to make two pumps that worked properly. At this time Emma gave him some good advice.

"Now, listen, Homer," she said. "Don't run off like a wild

man. You've got a good machine there, and I'm proud of you. But the Sarkhanese won't use it immediately just because it's good. Go slowly. Let them use the machine themselves, and in their own way. If you try to force them, they'll never use it."

"Well, tell me what to do," Atkins said. He knew she was right. He was grateful to her.

Emma calmly explained her plan to Homer. He understood that she had been thinking of this for some time. It was a beautiful plan. He wished that some of the government men could have heard it. He started to use the plan on the next day.

He drove in his jeep to the small village of Chang Dong. A hundred people lived there in fifteen or twenty houses. The village was built on a steep hill sixty miles outside Haidho. The soil there was rich, but it was a poor village. The work of raising water to the terraces was terribly hard. They were so high above the river that it took a long time. All the men were always tired in Chang Dong.

Atkins politely asked where the home of the headman was. He talked to the headman, who was seventy-five; and he talked in his own language. The headman was pleased that Atkins knew the language. During their talk he helped Atkins to find the proper words.

Atkins told the headman that he was an American engineer. He said that he had made a new kind of pump. This could lift water to the terraces, and he wanted to develop it. He did not try to explain about the piston and the cylinder; this man was not an engineer. He said that he wanted to make and sell pumps. He wanted the headman to find a clever Sarkhanese. He needed a man who knew something about machines. Atkins said that he would pay well for this man's time and skill. The man would also share the profits of the business.

The old man understood clearly, and they began to discuss the new mechanic's pay. Both the headman and Atkins were soon satisfied. They shook hands, and the headman went off to bring the mechanic.

He returned with a small man who looked very strong. His

name was Jeepo. He had been given this name because he could repair jeeps very well. Atkins did not listen very closely to the headman's words. He was studying the mechanic and he liked the man's looks.

Jeepo's hands were as dirty as Atkins' own hands. Jeepo looked steadily back at Atkins. In the mechanic's world of pistons and cylinders, they would work well together. That was clear enough. Jeepo was also as ugly as Atkins was. The two men smiled at one another.

"The headman says you're a good mechanic," Atkins said. "Have you ever worked on anything except jeeps?"

Jeepo smiled. "I've worked on pumps, cars, bicycles, and a few aircraft."

"Did you always understand everything that you did?"

"Does anyone understand everything?" Jeepo asked. "I think I can work on any machine. But that's only my own opinion. Try me."

"We'll start this afternoon," Atkins said. "There's a lot of stuff in my jeep outside. We'll take it off the jeep and start without delay."

By the middle of the afternoon they had done a lot. Twenty feet of bamboo pipe had been fixed together. The bottom of the pipe was put into the river near the village. The top part of the pipe was fixed into the pump which Atkins had planned. The frame of an old bicycle was placed above the pump. Both of its wheels had been taken off. Jeepo had put these things together himself, without Atkins' help. Everything was ready in the late afternoon.

Atkins drank some beer, and waited calmly. The headman and two or three others were sitting beside him. He could feel that they were very excited. They understood the purpose of the machine; but they did not believe that it would work.

"Sir, the machine is ready," Jeepo said quietly. "I'm ready myself to turn the pedals of the bicycle. Then we can see whether it works."

Atkins agreed. Jeepo climbed on the bicycle and began to

Jeepo climbed on the bicycle

turn the pedals. The pump worked slowly. Jeepo turned the pedals faster. The chain moved faster, and the pipes made strange noises. For several seconds there was no other sound. Then suddenly some dirty brown water rushed out of the top of the pipe. Jeepo did not stop pedalling or smile; but the headman and the others were very excited.

"This is a very clever machine," the headman said to Atkins. "In a few minutes you have lifted a lot of water. It is more than we can lift in five hours."

Atkins did not reply. He was waiting for Jeepo. He had a feeling that Jeepo was not entirely satisfied.

Jeepo continued to turn the pedals, and looked down at the machine. He saw that some changes ought to be made. He called out to Atkins to tell him about them. When the small field was covered with water, he got off the frame of the bicycle.

"It's a very clever machine, Mr. Atkins," Jeepo said. "But it is not a machine for this country."

Atkins looked at him steadily. "Why not?" he asked.

Jeepo did not immediately reply. He moved silently round the machine; then he stopped and faced Atkins.

"The machine works well," he said. "But a man who wants one must have a second bicycle. In this country, Mr. Atkins, very few people possess two bicycles. They haven't enough money. Unless you can find another way to drive the pump, your clever machine is useless."

For a moment Atkins felt angry. But he remained calm when he remembered Emma's advice.

"What happens to all the old bicycles in this country?" he asked Jeepo. "Aren't there enough of them to drive the pumps?"

"There are no old bicycles in this country," Jeepo said. "We ride bicycles until they fall to bits. When a man throws his bicycle away, it's too old for anything else."

"So what would you do, Jeepo?" Atkins asked. "You're a clever mechanic. You ought to have some ideas."

For a time Jeepo gave no answer. He sat in the field and

looked at the strange machine. He said nothing for ten minutes. Then he stood up and walked slowly to the machine. He turned the pedals and watched. Then he walked back to his place in the field.

The headman felt rather anxious, and watched Atkins' face. Jeepo was acting proudly. The headman told the others that after this no one would respect them. When Jeepo heard this, his ears changed to a red colour.

Atkins wanted to laugh. He walked towards Jeepo and sat down beside him. For fifteen minutes the two men sat quietly, studying the machine. Atkins spoke first.

"Perhaps we could make a wooden frame," he said.

"The frame's cheap enough," Jeepo answered. "It's the other parts that cost the money."

For ten more minutes they sat together. The headman and the others were talking all the time, but Atkins said nothing. Once he walked to the machine and turned the pedals. He and Jeepo thought of six answers to their problem, but each one was useless.

When darkness was falling, Jeepo suddenly stood up. He walked to the bicycle, and began to pedal hard. Water rushed out of the top of the pipe. He shouted ideas at Atkins.

He suggested that another frame ought to be made. It could be built of bamboo. This frame must be made to hold an ordinary bicycle. Then its back wheel could drive the pump. They would have to change the machine a bit. Then, after that, everything would be easy. Each family had a bicycle for use on the roads. This could be put into the bamboo frame, and then it would drive the pump. One bicycle could do both things. The family could use it both for travelling and for pumping.

Atkins showed his pleasure. "This mechanic has made a great discovery," he told the headman. "A bicycle can be used on the roads and also for the pump. Jeepo's idea has made everything possible. He must get half of the profits that will come out of this business."

The headman spoke a few words to the other men; then he turned to Atkins.

"Do you propose that you and Jeepo should build pumps together?" he asked.

"Yes. I want to enter into business with Jeepo. We'll start a factory and build this kind of pump. We'll sell the pumps to anyone who'll buy them. The man who buys will not need to pay the whole price immediately. He can pay over three years for his pump. Jeepo will have to work hard. He'll have to work as hard as I do myself."

The old men did not seem sure that Atkins would work hard. There was a lot of argument, but Jeepo himself said nothing. He stood by the machine and touched it. Then he left it. He spoke to the headman.

"I've listened to all of you, and I've said nothing," he said. "You're all foolish old men. This American knows how to work with his hands. He built this machine with them. You people do not understand machines; but Mr. Atkins and I understand each other. I will enter into business with him if he's ready to accept me."

The headman looked quite ashamed. "Jeepo's quite right," he said. "We can trust this American."

"When we've made some pumps," Atkins said, "we'll print some small books about them. These will explain how to make the pumps. We'll send them into all parts of the country. The village of Chang Dong will become famous."

Two days later Jeepo and Atkins rented a building just outside the village. They hired twelve men to do the work. They bought the necessary tools and materials, and in a week the work was going on well. A small sign was put up over the door: *The Jeepo-Atkins Company Limited*. Jeepo and Atkins worked eighteen or twenty hours a day. They trained other men and tested materials. They worked hard and became angry. They used bad language and hammered.

Emma Atkins moved from Haidho to the village of Chang Dong. She bought food in the village and cooked it at home.

She took food to the factory, and the other women of the village did the same. Once an important man came to the factory and spoke seriously to Atkins. Sarkhanese men, he said, must not handle machines. They had never done that before, and they must not do it now.

Atkins said exactly what he thought. The visitor drove away in his car with a red face and angry looks. Atkins went happily back to his work.

At the end of six weeks they had manufactured twenty-three pumps. When the twenty-fourth pump was ready, Atkins called the men together. Jeepo faced them with him.

"We are now coming to the difficult part of this business," Jeepo said. "You have worked well to make these pumps; but now you have to sell them. Each of you must take two pumps and go out to get orders. Try to sell the next pumps that we shall make. Show the two that you have. When you sell a pump, you'll be given a tenth of its price."

The men liked this plan very much indeed. It was new to them, but they were quite ready to try it. The next morning twelve carts stood outside the factory. Two pumps were loaded on each cart. By twelve o'clock every cart had gone to some part of the country.

Those who remained had now to wait. They knew that they must get some orders for pumps. The factory was useless without orders. The factory was now very important to the people of Chang Dong, and they did not want to close it.

Four days passed, but none of the men returned. A grey mist of sadness sank down on those who were waiting. Then, on the fifth morning, one of the men returned.

He was driving his cart at high speed, which is difficult. The ox which was pulling it almost fell down. Mud flew through the air as the wheels turned. Everyone in the village rushed to the factory. Everyone wanted to know what was going to happen next. The cart was covered with mud. It was empty.

The man who had driven it back got down slowly from his

They shouted with joy

seat. He was important, and he knew it. He walked calmly towards Jeepo and Atkins, and stood there in front of them.

"I wish to inform you, sirs, that I have done wrong," he said. A slow smile spread over his face. "You told me to bring back the two pumps, but I could not do so. I have received orders for eight pumps; but two of the men wanted their pumps immediately. They needed water terribly; the crops were almost dying. I did not want to give them the pumps, but I had to do that. I hope I have not made a bad mistake!"

Everyone in the crowd turned and looked at Jeepo and Atkins. Those two dirty men looked at each other for a moment. Then suddenly they shouted with joy. The whole crowd began to shout with joy. Everyone in the village was filled with happiness. A party started, and the whole village went to it.

The next morning everyone got up early. The first to rise were Jeepo and Atkins. Soon the sound of hammers could be heard in the factory. People went there and looked in. Jeepo and Atkins were in the middle of a violent argument; they were discussing changes in the plan of the pump. At the same time Emma Atkins was laying out an immense breakfast in front of the two men; but they were taking no notice of the food.

The argument continued loudly.

HILARY'S AUNT
Cyril Hare

Cyril Hare is the pen-name of His Honour Judge Alfred
Alexander Gordon Clark, born in 1900. He was educated at
Rugby School and at New College, Oxford. His books include
an important work on the law, but he is more famous for his
stories.

Hilary, the chief character in this short story, is a member
of a good family. Its great name, based on years of virtue and
correct living, is put into danger by Hilary. When he wants to
buy something, he writes a cheque to pay for it; unfortunately
he has no money in the bank, and the cheque is worthless. To
escape the laughter of other good families, and to escape the
danger of Hilary's being sent to prison, he is sent to Australia by
his angry father. Australia likes him no better than Britain did,
and when his father and brother die, he returns.

His father has sometimes mentioned an aunt, who appears
to have done something shameful. This secret is now made
plain: his aunt fell in love with a man who earned his living by
trade. Trade (buying and selling goods) was avoided by men of
good family, and gentlewomen were not expected to marry
shopkeepers. They had to marry men of other good families,
or men who were in one of the learned professions. This aunt,
therefore, did something terrible and was considered dead by
the rest of the family; but when Hilary came back from
Australia, he had to depend on her because he soon spent all
the family money.

In many good short stories, the reader finds something
unexpected near the end. Judge Gordon Clark uses his
knowledge of the law to provide the surprise in this one.

"The Victorian age", mentioned in the first few lines, refers
to the years when Victoria was queen (1837–1901). At that
time all good Britons behaved very correctly. Hilary's father
was Victorian in character, but Hilary himself was not.

HILARY SMITH belonged to a good family, and his father never hesitated to mention this fact. The actual age of the family was doubtful, but Mr. Smith behaved like a man of the past. His ideas and manners were those of the Victorian age.

Unfortunately Hilary himself had some unimportant trouble with the bank about a few cheques. It seemed a very slight matter to the young man, but not so to his father. Hilary was sent off to Australia without delay. Mr. Smith knew little about that place, but he understood one thing. It was a convenient country for those who did not like the customs of old England.

Hilary did not like Australia, and Australia did not like Hilary. He therefore took the earliest opportunity of returning to England. He could not, of course, earn enough money to buy a ticket. So he had to wait until his father and his brother died. They fortunately did this at the same time. After that he received all the money which belonged to the good old family.

There was not a great deal of money, and Hilary soon spent it. (The old family had not been able to get much in recent years.) When all the money had been spent, Hilary could do one of two things. He could die or work. The thought of neither of these gave him any pleasure. Then he remembered that he was not alone in the world. He possessed an aunt.

She was his father's only sister, and he knew little about her. His father's ancient ideas were responsible for this unfortunate fact. When her name was mentioned, he never looked very pleased. "Your aunt Mary brought no honour to the family," he said. Hilary, of course, tried to discover what she had done. It seemed that she had failed to marry a nobleman. Instead, she had chosen a husband who was connected with "trade". No old family could bear that sort of thing, of course. As soon as she became "Mrs. Prothero", her brother considered her dead. Later on, Mr. Prothero died and left her a lot of money; but that did not bring her back to life in her brother's opinion.

Hilary discovered his aunt's address by talking to the family lawyer. Fortunately she had remained faithful to him even after she fell. So Hilary's sun shone again, and the old lady seemed to like him. When he was feeling honest, he could talk attractively. He frequently visited his aunt's house; and soon he was living comfortably in the building which the profits of trade had provided.

Hilary was very relieved when he was able to move into the house. He felt like a sailor who had just reached harbour. He had only about sixpence in his pocket.

One thing was immediately clear: his aunt was seriously ill. She acted bravely, but she was slowly dying. He had a private talk with her doctor which alarmed him greatly. The doctor told him that nothing could cure the old woman. She might perhaps live for some time, but the end was certain.

"Her condition may become worse at any moment," the doctor said. "When it has passed a certain stage, she won't want to live. No kind person will want her to live either."

Hilary was very annoyed. Fate had found a home for him, and was now going to throw him out of it. Once again he would have to live in the hard world alone. There was only one thing that he could do. He chose an evening when his aunt was feeling better than usual. Then, very gently, he asked for details of her will.

When she heard the word "will", his aunt laughed loudly.

"Have I made a will?" she said. "Yes, of course I have. I left all my money to—now, what was it? To whom did I leave it? Some religious people in China, I think. Or were they in Polynesia? I can't remember. Blenkinsop, the lawyer, will tell you about it. He still has the will, I suppose. I was very religious when I was a girl."

"Did you make this will when you were a girl, Aunt Mary?"

"Yes, when I was twenty-one. Your grandfather told me to make a will. He believed that everyone ought to do that. I had no money then, of course, and so my will wasn't very useful."

Hilary had been filled with sorrow when he heard the first details; but now his eyes were happier again.

"Didn't you make another will when you were married?" he asked.

His aunt shook her head. "No," she said. "There was no
need. I had nothing and John had everything. Then, after John
died, I had a lot of money but no relations. What could I do
with the money?" She looked at Hilary with steady eyes.
"Perhaps I ought to talk to Mr. Blenkinsop again," she
suggested.

Hilary said that there was no need to hurry. Then he
changed the subject.

On the next day he went to the public library and examined
a certain book. It told him what he already believed. When a
woman marries, an earlier will loses its value. A new will must
be made. If no new will is made, the money goes to the nearest
relation. Hilary knew that he was his aunt's only relation. His
future was safe.

After a few months had passed, Hilary's problems became
serious. The change in his aunt's condition showed that the
doctor had been right. She went to bed and stayed there. It
seemed certain that she would never get up again. At the same
time Hilary badly needed money. He had expensive tastes, and
owed a lot of money to shopkeepers. They trusted him because
his aunt was rich; but their bills were terrible.

Unfortunately his aunt was now so ill that he could not
easily talk to her. She did not want to discuss money matters
at all. She was in great pain and could hardly sleep; so she
became angry when money was mentioned. In the end they
had a quarrel about the small amount of ten pounds. She
accused him of trying to get her money.

Hilary was not very angry. He understood that Aunt Mary
was a sick woman. She was behaving strangely because she was
ill. He remembered the doctor's words, and began to wonder
about a new problem. Was it kind to want his aunt to live any
longer? Was it not better for her to die now? He thought about
this for a long time. When he went to bed, he was still
thinking.

His aunt gave him some news in the morning. She told him
that she was going to send for Mr. Blenkinsop.

She accused him of trying to get her money

So she was going to make a new will! Hilary was not sure that a new will would help him. She might leave all her money to someone else. What could he do then? He reached a clear decision. He must do a great kindness to the poor old woman.

Every night she took some medicine to make her sleep. Hilary decided to double the amount. He did not need to say anything to her about it. He could just put her to sleep for ever.

He found that it was a very easy thing to do. His aunt even seemed to help his plans. An old servant had been nursing her, and she told this woman to go out. So the servant went off to attend to her own affairs. She was told to prepare the medicine before she went out. Then Hilary could give it to his aunt at the proper time.

It was easy for Hilary. He had only to put some more medicine into the glass. If anything awkward happened, he could easily explain. He could say that he had not understood the plan. He had not known that the servant had put the medicine in. So he had put the proper amount into the glass. It was unfortunate, of course. The total amount was too great. But who would suspect dear Hilary?

His aunt took the glass from his hand with a grateful look.

"Thank you, Hilary," she said. "I want, more than anything, to sleep, and never to wake up again. That is my greatest wish." She looked at him steadily. "Is that what you wish, Hilary? I have given you your chance. Forgive me if I am suspecting you wrongly. Sick people get these ideas, you know. If I am alive tomorrow, I shall do better for you. Mr. Blenkinsop is coming here, and I shall make a will in your favour. If I die tonight, you'll get nothing. Some people in China will get all the money. I ought, perhaps, to explain. John Prothero never married me. He already had a wife and couldn't marry again. That made your foolish father very angry with me . . . No, Hilary, don't try to take the glass away. If you do that, I shall know; and I don't want to know. Good-night, Hilary."

Then, very carefully, she raised the glass to her lips and drank.

TWO WEEKS BEYOND SHOREDITCH
Robert Rubens

This is the first story by Robert Rubens to appear in print (1965); but when he was writing it, he was also writing a full-length book.

Two Weeks Beyond Shoreditch appeared in *Winter's Tales 9*, a book which contained stories by nine other writers. Rubens has also been responsible for a rival book of short stories, *Voices 1*.

This story describes a visit to a hospital beyond Shoreditch. (Shoreditch is in east London, and is in a poor part of the city. It manufactures boots, shoes and furniture.) The man spends two weeks in the hospital. He finds a number of difficulties, and complains about them. Among the doctors who visit him is the great Dr. Dillman. Dr. Dillman criticizes him for complaining, and so the sick man orders him out of his room. This is most unusual. He almost has to leave the hospital; but he apologizes and is allowed to stay. The rest of the story describes part of the daily life of the hospital; and the people who work in it.

A word may be said about two parts of London which are mentioned in the story. Mile End and Stepney are also in the east part of London, north of the River Thames. Stepney contains the Tower of London, the main offices of the port of London, and the Royal Mint, the building in which British and other coins are made. Clothes are also made in Stepney and Mile End.

I WAS SICK for the whole day. When I looked at myself in the glass, I saw a grey face. I was like a dead body. So I went to Harley Street to see my doctor. I was too ill to think about the cost of the visit.

Dr. Franklin Roth took a quick look at me and made the usual tests. He told me that I had it; yes, I had jaundice.

"Jaundice?" I cried.

"Yes. Complete rest in hospital for four weeks," he said.

I told him that I could not afford an expensive place. He telephoned to several places and I heard the word "jaundice" every time. He found me a bed in a hospital somewhere beyond Shoreditch.

I took a taxi back to my room, where I picked up some clothes and a few books. Then I went to Shoreditch. It was a cold grey day, and the hospital looked terrible. It was built of red bricks and had rows of high little windows.

A tall Indian, who spoke very exactly, examined me. He pushed his fingers into my stomach. He asked me how old I was; he wanted to know the dates of all my old illnesses. I was too weak to talk much.

"When you were a boy," he said, "did you have this disease or that disease?" I answered him very shortly.

They wrapped me up in something warm and I was taken to another part of the hospital. My room was called a cubicle. It was on the ground floor and through its window I could see some grass. I got into bed in the cubicle and fell asleep immediately.

I woke up hours later. Sunlight was pouring over me, and voices could be heard in the hall. The cubicle had glass walls which separated me from other infectious men. It was like lying in a shop window. People walked slowly past, and looked in carelessly at me. There were two glass doors, and I saw some curtains on them; but the curtains were pulled back, and so I got out of bed to close them. Suddenly a very small nurse rushed in.

"You mustn't get out of bed," she said.

"I just wanted to draw the curtains."

"Curtains are not allowed to be drawn in the day-time. You must stay in bed. This rule is for infectious people. They stay in bed at all times."

She arranged the bedclothes. "Never get out of bed here," she said. She marched out of the cubicle.

My mouth was dry and I looked round for some kind of bell. I wanted to call the nurse back, but there was no bell. I saw her rushing through the hall, and I waved to her. She gave me one look and walked past the door. She saw me clearly, but did not come in. There was a tap in the corner of the cubicle, and so I waited. Soon I was sure that nobody was looking. I got out of bed and took some water from the tap.

"I told you before that you are not allowed out of bed." She had caught me.

"I had to have a drink of water."

"That tap is not for you. It is for doctors and nurses. They have to wash their hands before leaving the cubicle. You are infectious, and you must not use that tap."

"But I tried to catch your attention. You saw me waving, didn't you?"

"I am on afternoon duty now. I'm busy. Drinking water is given at tea time. It is not my work. You must ask another nurse." She arranged the bedclothes, washed her hands at the tap, and marched out.

"Well, good afternoon. Is everything all right?" A young man with a sharp nose was standing by the door. He had absolutely no hair. His hands were held together as if he was praying.

I rolled over to the other side of the bed. "No," I said.

"Oh, I'm sorry," he said. "What's the trouble?"

"That nurse is the trouble. She wants to hurt; she likes giving pain. Tell her to stay out of this cubicle."

"But she has to come in here. It's her work."

"She comes in and she's very rude. She wouldn't even bring me a glass of water. She said I must ask at tea time."

"I'm sorry about that." He looked confused. "I'll speak to her."

He fixed the curtain and looked out of the window. Then he started praying again and left.

A woman came in to clean the cubicle. "That's Mr. O'Fay," she said. "He's in charge here – such a nice man!" She was wearing a dull green dress and cap. She cleaned the entire cubicle in a few minutes. Before she left, she turned to speak. She spoke like someone from the middle of Europe.

"It's all right," she said. "It's not bad here after a time."

Evening came with a special meal for someone with jaundice. There was no fat in the food: only some cold wet chicken. They gave me a cold drink an hour later, and the lights went out. The next morning someone shook my arm at six o'clock and put a cup of tea on the table.

Then, an hour later, another nurse arrived. I hadn't seen her before. She gave me a wash with some water which was almost cold. Wonderfully she kept the bed dry; but I was soon as cold as ice.

I told myself that it was all Dr. Roth's fault. While I was thinking about him, Mr. O'Fay came in. He brought with him an Indian doctor called Laipul. Another man came too, a Dr. Dillman. He seemed to be important. He was one of those who were in charge of the whole hospital.

They stood at the foot of my bed while Mr. O'Fay closed all the curtains They had a look at my chest.

"Good morning, and how are you today?" said Dr. Dillman. He was fat and about seventy.

"I feel terrible," I said.

"Yes, you are a bit yellow, aren't you? But not severely so." He put his thumb under my eye and examined my chest. He said something softly to himself. He felt my stomach and wrote a note in his notebook. He whispered to Laipul.

"Mr. O'Fay has told me that you've complained about a nurse. Is that true?" Dillman was standing at the foot of the bed.

"Yes, I did complain about her. She was rude and unhelpful."

"Nobody has ever complained before about our nurses. This one especially has a spotless record. I think you made a mistake. You imagined that she was rude to you. People who are ill often imagine things."

The blood was beating in my head. "That's the important thing," I said. "I am ill, and she hasn't been helpful at all. She was very rude."

"When people have jaundice, they easily get angry. You must understand that."

"I'm sure you're right," I said. "Therefore a nurse ought to be more helpful than usual."

"I have every reason to believe that this is a very good nurse."

"How do you know?" I asked. "Has she ever taken care of you when you were ill? I'm telling you she's rude. She won't do anything to help. I don't want her in here again."

"We cannot change our plans just to suit you." He was looking straight at me. "I want you to apologize to her."

"I will not apologize to her. I did nothing wrong."

"She deserves an apology from you. You've made her angry."

"I've made *her* angry? What are you trying to do? Do you always fight those who come into this hospital?"

"You're not the sort of young man that I like," he said.

"Oh!"

"And I don't want your sort of person in here."

"And I don't want you in my cubicle," I cried. "This is my cubicle. So get out! All of you!"

Mr. O'Fay was anxiously pressing his hands together when he led the two doctors out.

I didn't know what would happen next. I was quite frightened. I did not really want to stay there; but probably it was as good as any other hospital. I didn't like the idea of changing at that time.

The next day Dr. Roth came in wearing a white coat. "This

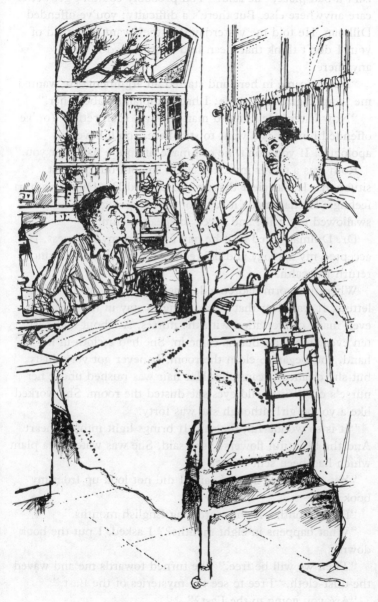

'This is my cubicle so get out!'

isn't a bad place," he said. "You probably couldn't get better care anywhere else. But there's a difficulty: you've offended Dillman. He told me yesterday that they want to get rid of you. I don't think that I can find another bed for you anywhere."

"But he came in here and started an argument. He wanted me to apologize to a nurse; I had complained about her."

"Now listen. He's an old man and will soon retire. You've offended him. If you want to stay here, you'll have to apologize. If you don't, he can make life quite nasty for you."

Roth was a clever man. He could smooth out difficult situations. It was clear that he had calmed Dr. Dillman's hurt feelings. He had made it easy for me to apologize. So I swallowed my pride and asked to speak to him.

Dr. Dillman acted as if he had forgotten my rudeness. He accepted my apology and offered his best wishes for a quick return to health.

When the storm had ended, I began reading and writing letters. It was clear that I was going to stay in the hospital. I even made conversation with the nurses. At about half past ten every morning Bertha came in. She had a cloth in her hand, and began to clean the room. It never got very dusty, but she cleaned it carefully. Her hair was pushed under her nurse's cap. With wild eyes she dusted the room. She worked like a young girl although she was forty.

"It is so wonderful, the sun. It brings light into my heart. And the beautiful flowers!" she said. She was watering a plant which had been sent to me.

"Yes, it's a nice day," I said. I did not look up from my book.

"Eight months. Eight more long English months."

"What happens in eight months?" I asked. I put the book down.

"Then we will be free." She turned towards me and waved the dust-cloth. "Free to see the mysteries of the East."

"Are you going to the East?"

"Yes. But I must wait first for my property. Every day I write to my mother in Salzburg to ask the date. But now I know it will be in eight months."

"Why in eight months?"

"Because she is selling it for me. It is property from before the war. It is my own property. I don't want to keep it in Salzburg. It is not my home any more."

"How long have you been away?" I asked.

"Seven years. When I go back, it is like visiting a foreign country. It is not the same Austria. It was different when I was a child. I hate going back." She was rubbing part of the window.

"For three years I worked in a house in Wales. I was studying all the time. I must always improve my mind. Even now I go to night classes. When I get my property, I will stop working here. I will study all the time. Perhaps I study too much; but I want to learn."

She went quietly out of the room.

"You're not as yellow as you were," said Mr. O'Fay. His voice was as high as usual. "Laipul said you've got jaundice mildly. You might only have to stay two weeks."

"Well, I'm glad to hear that," I said.

"I'm very tired today," said O'Fay. "I only had four hours' sleep last night. I moved into a new flat and stayed up until half past four. I was putting things in their places."

"Where's the flat?" I asked.

"In Stepney. It has its furniture, but there are no dishes. We had to go out and buy some."

"Are you sharing the flat?"

"Yes. I can't live alone. If I tried that, it would drive me mad. I lived here in the hospital for two years; but it wasn't like living alone. There was always someone here. I could meet people and talk to them."

He looked through the glass and saw Dr. Laipul; so he said that he would come back later. After he left I slowly settled myself down. I picked up my book and began to read. Then I heard screams from the next cubicle. I saw through the glass wall a little boy. He was jumping up and down on his bed and screaming. George, the orderly, was shouting at him.

George came from Spain. He put the boy into the bed by force. Then he came into my cubicle.

"That Tommy is mad," the orderly said. "He has been here too long. That is why he screams like that. Eight weeks in that cubicle. Like an animal in a cage. But he's a tough little animal. He's strong and he can scream well."

"Why has he been here so long? What's the matter with him?"

"He's being observed. The doctors are watching him. He has been ill, and they're not satisfied."

George was short and had hair like an Italian.

"Bad place for children," he said. "Bad place for anyone. How long are you going to stay here?"

"About two weeks more."

"Two weeks. No! It takes a long time. Get used to this place. If you don't, you'll soon be like Tommy. You'll be screaming like the boy. How did you get jaundice? Do you know? Too much drink? Do you drink a lot?"

"No, not much," I said. "Isn't it some germ that a man picks up?"

"Yes, yes. But where did you pick it up?" The orderly ran out of the cubicle.

After Tommy's screaming, I did not want to read any more. I turned over and over in the bed. I wrote a foolish letter to someone I had almost forgotten. I hadn't seen him for years. The great event of the day was lunch. It was a dull meal of fish.

The afternoons seemed endless. Tommy was always turning over and over in front of me. A few visitors came to see me. They were allowed to stay for half an hour, and they had to wear long white coats. The radio helped me a bit.

I began waiting anxiously for Bertha's visits. She used to march into the cubicle with a joyful face. She praised the beauty of England, the joys of learning and the wonders of travel. She watered the plant and talked about the gardens of Austria. She pretended to dust the room while she was talking. She told me about her walking trips through the mountains. She described her university days in Heidelberg. She had hoped then to be a doctor. She never once looked at me straight in the eyes. She looked at the curtains or at her fingers.

"Four times my fiancé was in the hospital," she said. "Now he can only lie in bed."

"What did your fiancé do before he was ill?" I asked.

"He worked in a hospital, with electric machines. But for a long time he has not been well enough to work."

"When do you think you'll get married?" I asked.

"Soon. We will fix a date soon. When he's well again. I tell him we will take some of my money. I mean the money from my property. Then we can make a wonderful journey together. But he says no. He is a real English gentleman. He won't use my money. But when we are married I will persuade him. We will go to Japan."

She had brought a map of the East with her. We started planning her journey from Hong Kong to Korea. Every day we studied it together. We learnt the sizes of the towns and the places of interest. We studied the prices of hotels and restaurants. She had also brought me two books about Tokio from the hospital library. I read these carefully. I made a list of ancient buildings that she ought to visit. I marked them on the map of Japan. Bertha studied the list. One day she told me all the names on it from memory.

"He will love it," she said. "It will be wonderful for him. It will be like another world to him. If you see another civilization, you understand your own better. That is what I tell him; but he laughs at me. He won't laugh when he is in one of those wonderful buildings. It will make him a new person. My poor fiancé will become a lot better."

She held up a book about Thailand. She said, "I will read this tonight. Tomorrow you will help me to plan a journey in Thailand, won't you?"

One lazy afternoon I was lying in bed and thinking. I tried to understand why I enjoyed Bertha's visits. Then I saw Mr. O'Fay moving quietly towards my door.

"I've been talking to Bertha," he said. "She told me that she likes talking to you."

"Well, I like talking to her."

"She's a very kind woman," he said.

"Yes, she is."

"I feel sorry for her," said O'Fay.

"Why?"

"She's had a terrible life. She was in Austria during the war. Most of her family were killed."

"She likes living in England," I said. "And she'll be getting married soon."

"I'm not sure about that," he said. "I don't think her fiancé will marry her. He likes her, but he's not ready for marriage. He isn't that sort of man. He's got a good thing already, and he knows it."

"What do you mean?" I asked.

"She has been supporting him for the last three years. She has taken him all over Europe twice. Once she took him to visit her family in Austria. He stayed there six months and paid her mother nothing. Bertha had to come back to London to her work. She sent him half her pay every week. Then she sent him a ticket to come back."

"But he's ill, isn't he?" I said.

"Oh, yes, he's sick, but not very sick. He could do some light work if he wanted to. I was there last night, visiting them. He looked strong enough to me. He was sitting there and watching television. He was complaining about Bertha's cooking. In fact she's a good cook."

"What does he do all the time?"

"He just sits and watches the television. He reads stories while she's working here all day. They've been living in that room for three years."

"She thinks he's going to marry her soon."

"She's been thinking that for three years. If she didn't think that, she would be lost." He turned away. "Laipul's here now. I've got to go."

I suppose that I had understood some of this before. Bertha's talk about getting married was a dream; so was the journey to the East. Perhaps the property in Salzburg was a dream too. I felt sorry about it. I liked to think of her happiness. Mr. O'Fay's conversation had hit me quite hard. All my talks with Bertha were hollow now. I couldn't believe it all. I couldn't sleep that night, and I had to ask the nurse for some medicine.

The next morning Bertha marched in with joyful looks. "Now I have some new clothes," she said. "They are beautiful. I went yesterday to Mile End and bought them. I had seen them once in a shop weeks ago. They have little white flowers all over the cloth. I put them on for my fiancé to see. He said I look like a young girl."

"Did you buy a hat?"

"No. I took my old hat and put new flowers on it. It was easy. My fiancé smiled and smiled when he saw me in the dress. He is not a man who praises much; but yesterday I could see that he was pleased. He didn't even have to say so."

She watered the plant and touched it. "Yesterday was a good day for me. Everything was good. I had a new dress. My fiancé was happy. Then, after dinner, I went to watch television with George, the orderly. Mr. O'Fay came too. They have a nice flat."

"Do you mean Mr. O'Fay who works here?"

"Yes. He and George. You know the Spanish orderly. They have just moved into a flat together. It's nice and new. They're happy there."

She looked down the hall. She explained that she had not finished the Thailand book yet. As she was leaving, George rushed in. He began arranging my bed.

"You're still yellow," he said. "You look like a flower."

"Thank you. I love to hear it."

"But it's true. You get more yellow every day."

"Dr. Laipul says I'm improving," I said.

"Laipul's mad. He has bad eyes, and can't see. I'm telling you. You are yellow."

"George," I said, "could you do something for me?"

"I can do some things, but not everything. What is it, yellow boy?"

"Cigarettes."

"Cigarettes? You must ask Mr. O'Fay for permission. Do you think I want to lose my place here?"

"You won't lose it," I said. "I'll give you the money. I want a smoke."

"No, no, you must ask Mr. O'Fay. He's very severe about that." I had to wait an hour without cigarettes until O'Fay came in. He was pressing his hands together as usual.

"Of course he can get them for you," he said. I had told him that I needed some cigarettes. "He'll get them in the lunch hour. How are you feeling today?"

"Fine! How are you?"

"Not so good. I had a quarrel last night with my companion. The man who lives in the flat drives me mad. He gets up at three o'clock in the morning. He goes into the kitchen to cook. He says he can't sleep. I've got to have my rest. I have to be here at eight o'clock every morning. Besides that, he hasn't paid any rent yet. And all the food's mine. When he cooks things at three o'clock, it's my food. I bought it all."

"What did you do?"

"I told him to get out. I pay the rent; the flat's in my name. So I told him to go. I couldn't bear it any more. Now I have to pay six pounds a week myself; and living there alone drives me mad.

The orderly, George, walked in just then. They looked fiercely at each other. Then O'Fay took the water-bottle and left.

"What did he say?" George asked.

"He said you can get me the cigarettes."

"I knew he would say yes. But it's better to ask him. He's a nice man, but a little strange in the head. Don't you agree?"

Sometimes during the day, Mr. O'Fay and the orderly had to work together. This happened, for example, when they were getting meals ready. Mr O'Fay was tall, and walked unsteadily; he was like a thin tree in a strong wind. Together they reminded me of a priest and a young doctor.

But Mr. O'Fay looked paler than usual. He rushed from one cubicle to another and repeated the story of the flat. He wanted someone else to share his flat.

"It's driving me mad! I can't live alone. I have to take stuff to make me sleep."

Bertha came in. "Tomorrow," she said, "we shall arrange the journey through Thailand." Her face was red. She would be hearing the bells of Bangkok all the afternoon. I could see that.

"Have you talked to Mr. O'Fay today, Bertha?" I asked. "He's not very happy."

"I know. It's that devil, George. He stays up too late. But I must go now and finish my work. I have to go to the class."

George came in and threw the cigarettes on the bed. "I've had enough of England," he said. "I'll go to Germany and learn German. When I can speak English, French and German, then I can work in my father's restaurant."

"Is that what you're going to do?"

"What else should I do?" the orderly replied. "That is why I came here. I came to learn English so as to speak to tourists."

"Why have you had enough of England?"

"It is all stiff like the collars. When I first came, I liked London. It seemed mad and joyful. But it's not. It's sad like a funeral. I know some other boys from Spain who are here. Every night they go to coffee houses. They like that. They think London is wonderful. They all live in one little flat – eight of them. I don't like to live like that and just drink coffee."

"But why do you want to leave England?"

"The time has come. I speak English now, so I must leave. And I leave here now. I'm going to the cinema tonight to see Helen Shapiro. Good-night, yellow boy."

He rushed down the hall and passed Mr. O'Fay. They did not look at each other.

The next morning Bertha brought me my breakfast. "It's all finished," she said. "They've left the flat. It was a beautiful new flat and it had television."

"Do you mean George and Mr. O'Fay?"

"Yes. He made George move out. Now he is selling the dishes. That mad fellow, George, spends all his money on clothes. They are not friends any more. They don't even look at each other. It's terrible."

"I thought he was going to share the flat with someone else," I said.

"He thought so, pernaps. But now he's leaving it. He's coming back to the hospital. He ought not to work here and live here too. That's no good."

I saw George rushing in and out of the cubicles. He put his head inside my door.

"George, come here a minute," I said. "What have you decided to do?"

"I think I'll stay in England. I don't know why. I just think so. Perhaps tomorrow I'll change my mind."

Mr. O'Fay came in while I was eating lunch. "I'm leaving the flat," he said. "I'm coming back to the hospital."

"What happened to the other fellow?" I asked. "I mean the man who was sharing with you."

"Oh, he's gone to live with some wild men from Spain."

Bertha suddenly rushed in and gave me an envelope. It looked important. It came from a London office.

"It's happened!" she cried. "He's done it! He's going to marry me! Look at that envelope!"

"It's about a marriage!" I said, confused.

"Yes! I have to sign the paper. It's wonderful. I knew that it would happen soon. He wrote about it without telling me.

'It's happened!' she cried

It's a wonderful surprise. I'll have to go to the office and arrange everything. It takes ten days. This is the happiest day for me. In two weeks I'll be Mrs. Johnson."

I watched her running along the hall. She waved the letter and showed it to Mr. O'Fay. Then she showed it to George. I was glad that Mr. O'Fay was wrong about her fiancé. I was glad that the news of the marriage had come then. I was going to leave the hospital the following afternoon.

An hour later Bertha came in still holding the letter.

"Not for me," she said. "It says on the envelope: Bertha Bainer. They made a mistake and gave it to me. My name is Bertha Rainer. But it's all right. I know the other Bertha. She is also an Austrian who used to work here. Now she is at another hospital. I will take this to her tomorrow."

"I'm sorry to hear that," I said. "A terrible mistake."

"It's my fault," she said with a brave little smile. "I ought to have looked more carefully at the envelope. And we're not ready for marriage yet. It's better for us to wait. My property will soon be sold. It will be wonderful to have some money. How many interesting buildings are there in Thailand? Where is the map?"

I opened the map on which I had marked the journey. Bertha studied it for a moment and then watered the plant. I watched her pouring the water slowly into it.

"Bertha," I said, "do you want that plant?"

"But it is yours," she said.

"I don't want to take it home with me tomorrow. You must take it when I leave."

"You will give me this wonderful plant! It will bring light into my room. And my fiancé loves flowers very much."

On the next day I left the hospital. I was warned to lie down a lot. I was told not to stand very much for a week.

My room was just as I had left it two weeks before. I knew that I ought to stay at home. I ought to have gone to bed early, but a friend telephoned. He wanted me to go out to dinner, and I could not resist the invitation.

I felt weak on my feet, but I found a bus. I climbed to the top and lit a cigarette. As the bus moved along Heathdene Road, I recognized a familiar figure. Bertha was walking on the other side of the street. I only saw her for a moment, because the bus rounded a corner. She was still in her green clothes. She had taken off her cap, and her hair was streaming in the wind. She looked very young and determined. She marched up Heathdene Road. She was carrying my yellow plant and it was protecting her from the wind.

Exercises

1. In the story *The Dream*, notice: *Even if* warnings are possible, this dream had no sense in it.
   Complete the following sentences suitably:
   (a) Even if you press hard on the brake, you ...
   (b) Even if the car had struck the woman at the table, ...
   (c) Even if you had helped me, ...
   (d) Even if the car had had more powerful brakes, ...
   (e) Even if I had understood French well, ...

2. In the story *Dark they Were with Golden Eyes*, notice: The old records have all been lost. (Form B.) This means (We) have lost all the old records. (Form A.)
   Change the following from Form A to Form B, and put the adverbs in the right places:
   (a) He could hardly have broken the log even with a heavy axe.
   (b) He was almost forgetting the rocket.
   (c) The sun was always burning the land.
   (d) The men at the door of Sam's factory were just watching him.
   (e) In that case he might even have completed the rocket.
   (f) Mr. Bittering knew that Mars was slowly changing his bones.
   (g) He ought never to have spent all that time on the rocket.
   (h) The Martians had once built cities.
   (i) The water would eat away my flesh.
   (j) Ought they to have avoided the villas in the mountains for ever?

3. In the story *It Happened Near a Lake*, notice: She was afraid that he might enjoy himself. (*Might* is more uncertain than *Would*.)
   Complete the following sentences without using *Would*:
   (a) If he went to the lake, he ...
   (b) If they had had a village in Miami, ...? (Question.)
   (c) She was never afraid that ...
   (d) He thought that it ... be possible to find ...
   (e) If you ever got tired of wandering about, ...

4. In the story *The Ugly American and the Ugly Sarkhanese*, notice: The top part of the pipe was fixed into the pump which Atkins had planned.
   Complete the following sentences:
   (a) You have told us nothing about the roads which ...
   (b) The people need a factory which ...
   (c) The fields need water which they ...
   (d) They lived in a small cottage which they ...
   (e) The piston which ... came from a jeep.

5. In the story *Hilary's Aunt*, notice: Unfortunately his aunt was now so ill that he could not easily talk to her.
   Complete the following sentences suitably:
   (a) Hilary had so much trouble with the bank ...
   (b) His father had been so displeased with Aunt Mary ...
   (c) He visited his aunt's house so frequently ...
   (d) His aunt was so kind ...
   (e) She was in such great pain ...
   (f) So expensive were Hilary's tastes ...
   (g) His aunt was so seriously ill ...
   (h) The bills were so terrible ...
   (i) In early life she had been so religious ...
   (j) There was so much medicine in the glass ...

6. In the story *Two Weeks beyond Shoreditch*, notice: His hands were held together as if he was praying.
   Complete the following sentences suitably:
   (a) That nurse acts as if . . .
   (b) She spoke as if she . . .
   (c) Dr. Dillman walked into the cubicle as if . . .
   (d) Mr. O'Fay looked as if . . .
   (e) Dr. Dillman came in again and spoke as if . . .
   (f) Bertha cleaned the room as if . . .
   (g) (When I go back to Salzburg), it is as if I . . .
   (h) He was jumping up and down on his bed as if . . .
   (i) He is not a man who praises much; but yesterday he spoke as if . . .
   (j) My companion in the flat acts as if . . .

   In the same story notice: I wrote a foolish letter to someone (whom) I had almost forgotten.
   In the following sentences leave out *whom* or *which* if possible:
   (a) She watered the plant which someone had given me.
   (b) Roth could smooth out the difficult situations which arose.
   (c) The room which Bertha cleaned never got very dusty.
   (d) The money which she got from her property could pay for the journey.
   (e) The nurses whom we employ here have spotless records.
   (f) I cannot find another bed which would suit you.
   (g) The meal which they brought to me was dull.
   (h) Tomorrow we shall arrange the journey which we shall make through Thailand.
   (i) I gave her the plant which she liked.
   (j) The property which belongs to me will soon be sold.